Who Works Here?

Fast-Food Restaurant

by Lola M. Schaefer

Heinemann Library
Chicago, Illinois

© 2001 Reed Educational & Professional Publishing
Published by Heinemann Library,
an imprint of Reed Educational & Professional Publishing,
100 N. LaSalle, Suite 1010
Chicago, IL 60602
Customer Service 888-454-2279
Visit our website at www.heinemannlibrary.com

Designed by Wilkinson Design
Printed in Hong Kong

05 04 03 02
10 9 8 7 6 5 4 3 2

Library of Congress Cataloging-in-Publication Data
Schaefer, Lola M., 1950-
　　Fast-food restaurant / by Lola M. Schaefer.
　　　　p. cm. -- (Who works here?)
　　Includes bibliographical references and index.
　　ISBN 1-58810-125-8 (library binding)
　　1. Hospitality industry--Employees--Job descriptions--Juvenile literature. 2. Fast food
restaurants--Juvenile literature. [1. Fast food restaurants. 2. Occupations.] I. Title.

　　TX911.3.J65 S33 2001
　　647.94'023--dc21

00-058096

Acknowledgments
Photography by Phil Martin.
Special thanks to Kent Brown and the workers at Wendy's in Fort Wayne, Indiana, and to workers everywhere who take
pride in what they do.

Every effort has been made to contact copyright holders of any material reproduced in this book. Any omissions will be
rectified in subsequent printings if notice is given to the publisher.

Some words are shown in bold, **like this.**
You can find out what they mean by looking in the glossary.

Contents

What Is a Fast-Food Restaurant?

Millions of people eat at fast-food restaurants every day.

A fast-food restaurant is a **business** that makes, sells, and serves food quickly. Each restaurant prepares sandwiches, salads, potatoes, desserts, and drinks. The crew, working together, offers food to **customers** from morning until late at night.

The trained crew keeps the restaurant clean and tries to deliver food to the customer in less than a minute. People of all ages buy food at fast-food restaurants. The crew wants to please their customers so they will come back again.

This fast-food restaurant is in Fort Wayne, Indiana. The map shows the places where the people in this book work. Many fast-food restaurants in the United States look like this.

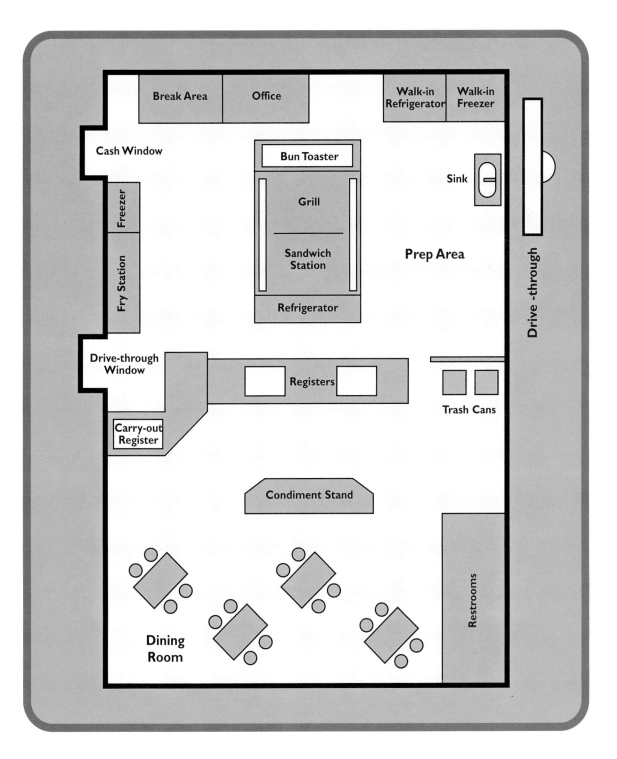

Area Director

An area director of fast-food restaurants is responsible for many stores in a large area. This person often visits the crew of each store. He or she checks that the restaurant is keeping **customers** happy and making money. If **employees** need further training, the area director will plan new programs to teach the necessary skills.

Mike is an area director. He is showing the correct way to cook and salt meat on the grill.

Here, Mike and the area supervisor are changing the crew's schedule.

Mike, like other area directors, is responsible for new restaurants. He chooses the location for each new store and oversees the **construction** of the building. It takes about 90 days to build and open a new fast-food restaurant. People work in the **business** many years before becoming an area director.

Area Supervisor

Chris, the area supervisor, is recording sales numbers from each of his restaurant managers.

An area supervisor is responsible for supporting each manager at several fast-food restaurants in one area. Together they record the number of sales at one restaurant in a week, month, and year. The area supervisor helps each manager keep the crew trained and working as a team.

Fast food means food prepared and served quickly. Area supervisors check the service time at the drive-through window. They time the crew as they listen to the order, prepare the food, sell the food, and hand it to the **customer.** Area supervisors want this service to be very fast.

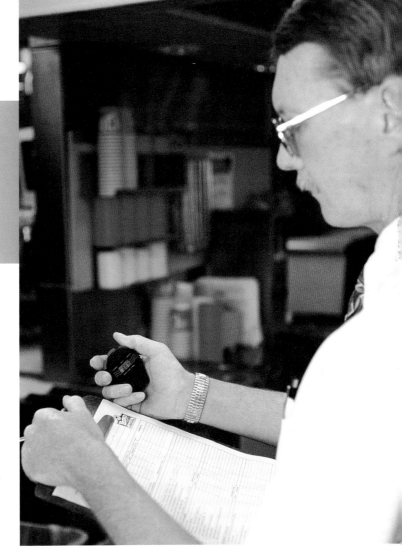

This area supervisor uses a stopwatch to record the service time at the counter.

Marketing Manager

The marketing manager, Kent, puts a new toy display in the **customer** walkway.

A marketing manager informs the **community** of new events or changes at the fast-food restaurant. This person places **advertisements** (ads) with the radio, newspapers, and television. These ads tell the public about special prices, new food items, or the opening of a new restaurant.

Marketing managers study **business** and marketing in college. Many also attend restaurant manager training for several weeks. Marketing managers use reading, writing, and speaking skills every day on the job.

Kent and the area supervisor are programming the register for a new sandwich.

Store Manager

A fast-food restaurant store manager sets up the cash registers each morning and shuts them down at night. He or she checks the **stock** on hand at the counters, in the kitchen, and in the back rooms. A store manager wants plenty of cups, bowls, dressings, and meat ready for quick **customer** service.

Angie is the manager of this store. She opens the restaurant each morning.

Angie counts the cheese in the walk-in refrigerator before she places an order.

Store managers have usually worked in fast-food restaurants for 1–3 years. The company gives them several weeks of manager training. During that time, they learn the different jobs in the store. They learn how to make all the different kinds of food. Store managers need good math skills to complete the daily paperwork and food orders.

Crew Leader

Stacey is a crew leader. This morning he is chopping beef to make chili.

Crew leaders come to work early and prepare the restaurant for **business.** They turn off the alarm system and turn on the lights and kitchen machines. Crew leaders cut, chop, and slice some of the foods for sandwiches and salads.

New crew leaders work with other crew leaders to learn the job. They help other members of the crew by answering questions. Crew leaders need to be organized and able to work well with people in order to oversee other **employees.**

Here, Stacey takes potatoes out of the oven. He will place them in heat drawers to keep them hot.

Register Operator

Register operators greet **customers** at the counter. They enter the customer's order using the register pad, and it shows up on **monitors** in the kitchen. While waiting for the food order, register operators prepare drinks. After the customer pays for the food, they give him or her a **receipt** and the tray of food.

Shawn is a register operator. Here, he serves an order to a customer.

Shawn toasts buns for sandwiches before the restaurant opens.

Shawn, like other register operators, trained at work for his job. He starts work early and helps mop floors and vacuum the carpets. Register operators always wash their hands before handling food. They also use special rags to **disinfect** the register area.

Using Drive-through Window Technology

This customer will receive fast service at the drive-through window.

When a car pulls up to the outside menu, it moves past a **motion detector.** This detector starts a timer in the store. It also rings a bell in each headset. The window operator answers the bell within seconds and takes the **customer's** order.

Each worker can control the **volume** of the headset using a dial on the battery pack.

The crew members can hear the customer's order through their headsets. A headset is like a wireless **walkie-talkie** that lets the crew speak or listen while using both hands to complete an order. As the customer drives away, another motion detector stops the timer. Service times are recorded on a computer so the crew can check the speed of their work.

Grill Operator

A grill operator also comes to work early. He or she helps clean the floors and kitchen. Before the restaurant opens, a grill operator turns on the grill to begin heating. When the grill is ready, the grill operator puts different pieces of meat on the grill to cook.

Luis is a grill operator. He washes the tile floor so **customers** will come into a clean restaurant.

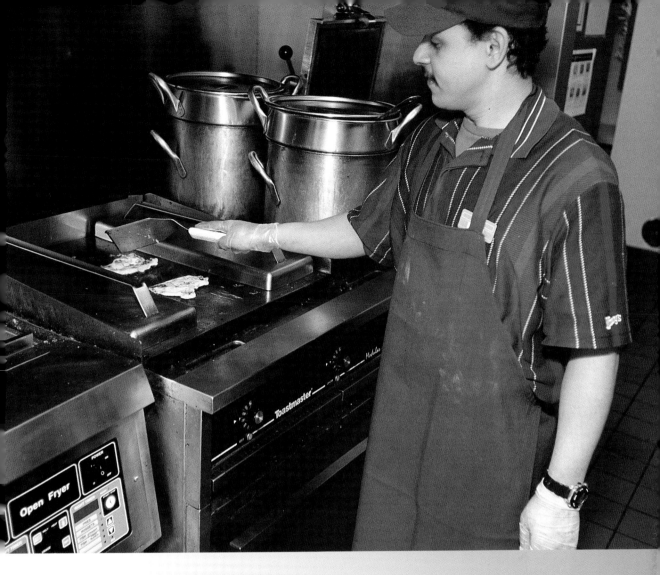

Luis is grilling chicken for the many lunchtime sandwiches being ordered.

Luis and other grill operators learn their skills on the job. They learn how to work the grill without getting burned and cook meat so it is safe to eat. During busy times, grill operators need to keep a full load of meat on the grill.

Sandwich Maker

Sandwich makers watch the kitchen **monitor** and listen with their headsets for **customer** orders. When a sandwich is ordered, sandwich makers pull down a wrapper, place a bun on top, add toppings and meat, and close the bun. They wrap the sandwich tightly and put it in the marked slide.

Fely, a sandwich maker, adds mustard to this cheeseburger order.

Sandwich makers, like Fely, touch the food they make. They must wear **latex** gloves to prevent the spread of germs. If sandwich makers leave their workstations, they need to wash their hands and put on new gloves. Restaurants that serve food must follow these important safety rules.

Fely wears gloves to keep the food clean and safe for customers.

HAND WASHING ZONE

STOP

& WASH YOUR HANDS

Fry Person

A fry person is responsible for cooking the different fried foods at the fry station. He or she may cook French fries, fish, and chicken nuggets in the fry baskets. A fry person works ahead so there are always a few orders ready to serve.

Bryant is a fry person. He is putting bags of frozen French fries into the **stock** cabinet.

Bryant uses a fry scoop to place French fries in the fry carton.

Working at the fry station is a hot job. Fry people cannot wear **latex** gloves because of the heat. It would melt the gloves. So fry people wash their hands often to prevent the spread of germs.

Using Fry Station Technology

A fry person touches the FRIES keypad to start the timer for three minutes.

After a fry person lowers a fry basket, he or she touches a keypad. Each keypad has been **programmed** to cook one type of food for a set time. Different foods cook in the vegetable oil as the timers run.

Buzzers sound in the kitchen when the different timers stop. The fry person pulls the fry baskets from the oil. He or she will let the cooked food drain for five seconds. Then, the fry person pours the food into a fry bin under the heat lamps.

This food will stay warm and fresh until it is needed for a **customer** order.

Dining Room Person

Karon, a dining room person, cleans a table between customers.

A dining room person works out front where **customers** sit and eat. This person keeps the dining room clean and free of germs. After removing trays and trash, he or she **disinfects** the tables. A dining room person also answers customers' questions.

Dining room people check and refill the **condiments** at the tables and on the condiment stand. They work hard to keep the dining room a pleasant place to eat. During birthday parties, dining room people help with food and fun.

This dining room person is refilling the plastic silverware on the condiment stand.

Glossary

advertisement (ad) public notice that gives information about an event or product

business company that makes, buys, or sells things

community area where people live, work, and shop

condiment seasoning for food; ketchup, pepper, and mustard are condiments

construction the act, process, or business of building something

customer person who shops and buys in a store or business

disinfect to make something free of germs

employee person who works for someone else and is paid to do so

latex milky liquid that comes from certain plants and can be used to make rubber

monitor visual display screen; like the screen on a computer

motion detector device that is programmed to do something because of movement

program put instructions or information into a computer to do a specific job

receipt piece of paper showing that money, goods, or a service has been received

stock all the items that a business needs

volume loudness

walkie-talkie radio used to talk short distances that is powered by batteries and small enough to be carried by one person

More Books to Read

An older reader can help you with these:

Chandler, Gil. *Getting Ready for a Career in Food Service.* Danbury, Conn.: Children's Press, 1995.

Gould, William. *McDonald's.* Lincolnwood, Ill.: NTC Contemporary Publishing Company, 1996.

Streissguth, Thomas. *Getting Ready for a Career in Food Service.* Minnetonka, Minn.: Capstone Press, Inc., 1996.

Index